Buying a Heart

By George MacBeth

Y0-BTZ-214

ATHENEUM   NEW YORK   1978

Library of Congress Cataloging in Publication Data
MacBeth, George.
Buying a Heart.

PR6063. A13B85   1977   821'.9'14   77-76755
ISBN 0-689-10816-8

Manufactured in Great Britain

First American Edition

CAVEN'S

Acknowledgements

Some of these poems have appeared in Ambit,
New Lines, New Poems I and II, The Pen Anthology
New Poems 1972, The Poetry Review, and the
Times Literary Supplement. Six were in pamphlets
published by the Fantasy Press, the Sceptre Press
and Turret Books, and one was in the American
edition of my book The Night of Stones.

CONTENTS

I

AN OLD STORY

During this period, the servants were getting divorced, and
life was far from easy at Satisfaction Cottage. Old Anxiety
left for ever, and Tom Quartz took to composing daily
bulletins to fill in his misplaced time.

Well, there was often dry liver on the mokko-plate that
always reminded M of the 1930s, and Tom heard him say once
it reminded him of his father to see *Bonny and Clyde*. But S.
had thought he was impotent, and was very tense through it.

Anyway, they got through December, Christmas being a sore feast
at the best of years, and this not one of those. Poor Tom
lay once in a near-coma, slashed in the thigh by Dorian
Filibuster in the spare garden.

On Boxing Day, the wind carried slates off the mansard roof,
and Slippers roamed merrily on the basement steps, awkward face
to the window unmolested. Such was the lowered state to which
all came, security dropped below the ramparts.

I doubt not Emery was to blame for some of this, but Tom Quartz
alone braved the winter to cuff the armadillo, run his colours
up the crab-apple, and call out Dorian in the killing-ground
beyond the robin's nest.

America wrote, but only once, and S. cried all night under the
steaming duvet, hearing the silver clink of solitude grow less
and less appetising in the bite of January. O January,
sidesman of plenty, you were slow coming!

Yes, the New Year. A freak Spring it was, with the plum-
blossom gyrating above the Norfolk stone before Santa had
barely packed his bags and driven North in his Emmenthal
Capri. But then it was late in a bad century.

So the Stock Market picked up, and all got better suddenly, in
the bleak aside of an agent's report: a decree absolute has

been observed at Highland Green, and may soon be over Almond Crescent. Alas, for that simplicity!

The belts of low pressure diminish, the kilted ladies derive no satisfaction from Tom Quartz in his bedside entertainments, nor does the mid-season bonsai, quartered in his office.

All grindeth to its own halt, as *The Saratogian* says, and the hint of February put a stop to all this shake-up in the corridors of a once-well-ordered mansion. Tom Quartz was glad of it, and he slept through much of March.

But the pair who had lain like spoons through twenty years in the square bed, lay there no more, and the ashes of orange Dick sifted through the atmospheres as in a bathysphere.

It was an old story, and no-one cared very much, except perhaps for the watchers in the shrubbery, the pink eyes of Fairbanks and the toad who had both come by surprise in their time to make a legend, and came no more.

Tom Quartz pricked up his ears, though, and cured that strawberry wound in his leg, and you see him now if you go up Vicinity Hill very smart in his gilt buttons and fraternity blazer, making the best of a poor bargain and eating chopped steak like a stevedore.

LAST NIGHT

I

Something that walked on air,
And curled in my chairs, has gone.
I saw its beautiful face
Grown lined with care and wan.

II

The poison was in its head,
I expect, before it came.
I never thought it could spread
And spoil our marvellous game.

III

It lived on silks, for a time.
It kept things in my drawers.
It would dig its nails in my skin.
Its ways were as sweet as a whore's.

IV

Its claws lay on my arm
As light as moss. It stirred,
And my air was what it breathed:
Its joy was what I heard.

V

It came to me in my room,
And it went, whenever it came.
Its long skin lay unrolled,
And that was always the same.

VI

Sometimes at dawn I would wake
And feel it warm on my back.
It had come close in the dark
Out of some sense of lack.

VII

And then, one October night
In an old house far away
I thought that I heard it cry,
And it wanted me to stay.

VIII

Outside the window I watched
The shapes of the oaks in the wind.
It was eating what it could,
But its flesh was wasted and thinned.

IX

Nothing could save it now,
Not even the taste of love.
I touched the infected flesh
That the long hair lay above.

X

It was all that I had to own.
Its fur was on all my sleeves.
I stooped, and kissed its face.
And it died, amidst the leaves.

TO WEEP

I

I ask the night sky, I ask the stars to weep.
I ask the hanging jackets in the bedroom cupboard
to weep.
I ask the filing cabinets in the little bedroom.
I ask the pot the fish is cooked in
in the kitchen to weep.
I ask the bowl of the lavatory.
I ask the porcelain of the hand-basin to weep.

II

I ask the remote dials in the dashboard of
the car to weep.
I ask the gutter.
I ask the snails in the long grass in
the park to weep.
I ask the black rabbit eloping with
her own shadow in the garden to weep.
I ask the toad.

III

I ask the darkness creeping out of the
ground to weep.
I ask the light.
I ask the pepper hinting at its own annihilation
in the sweet larder to weep.
I ask the sweating cheese.
I ask the spoons to weep.
I ask the delivered bottles of Glenfiddich
still wrapped in their Christmas cellophane.
I ask the milk to weep.

IV

I ask the sheets, I ask the pillow to weep.
I ask the spider below the skirting-board.

I ask the chamber-pot to weep.
I ask the ceiling.
I ask the spectacles in their case to weep.
I ask the boots with their broken zip.

V

I ask the wilderness in the mind of
the pony going to the slaughterhouse to weep.
I ask the blood raging.
I ask the solicitor with his gavel.
I ask the auctioneer on the chopping-block
to weep.
I ask the hangman selling knuckle-bones
to the proper authorities to weep.
I ask the skull.

II

BOREDOM

Somewhere (yes, I know where,
No, I won't tell you where)
Well-fed, warm and at ease
Lying late in a bed
Out of a window I
Watch a dead station-wall.
Scene one: nothing, as yet.

Next, through wet streets I walk,
Rinsed out after the rain.
Someone (no, I don't know
Who, but only her — yes)
Walks in front of me, well
Wrapped up after the rain.
Scene two: all right, you win.

Somehow (well, you know how,
You've been there in your time)
Women's fingers that lock
Lock and lock and lock. Well,
Then, upstairs to a room
Bang up against a wall.
Scene three: back as you were.

Scene four: (is there a fourth?
No, it just peters out).
Why does every affair
Sometimes (looking around
One's life) seem to involve
Just the same station wall
Seen from bed in the rain?

HOW TO EAT AN ORANGE

First you must roll it in your hands
To loosen the firm outer skin.
Peel this all off. Sealed perfume-glands
Fling their faint sweetness like a thin

Spray on scrubbed air. Palm-cupped, your sun,
Stripped, looks ripe to burst. First ease
Apart the packed liths: lightly run
Washed fingers in: then slowly squeeze

Bunched curves of it. Your joints get wet
With rippling juice: your pared nails meet
In wads of pith. It halves. You whet
Fresh appetite; but, set to eat,

Feel the rough tongue twist in your lips
And spit small, bitter, bone-dry pips.

AN ODE TO ENGLISH FOOD

O English Food! How I adore looking forward to you,
Scotch trifle at the North British Hotel, Princes Street,
Edinburgh. Yes, it is good, very good, the best in Scotland.

Once I ate a large helping at your sister establishment,
the Carlton Hotel on Waverley Bridge overlooking the cemetery on
Carlton Hill. It was rich, very rich and pleasant. O, duck, though

roast, succulent duck of the Barque and Bite, served with
orange sauce, mouth-meltingly delicious! You I salute. Fresh,
tender and unbelievable English duck. Such

luscious morsels of you! Heap high the groaning platter
with pink fillets, sucking pig and thick gammon, celestial chef.
Be generous with the crackling. Let your hand slip with the gravy
trough, dispensing plenty. Yes, gravy, I give you your due, too.
O savoury and delightsome gravy, toothsome over

the white soft backs of my English potatoes, fragrant
with steam. Brave King Edwards, rough-backed in your dry scrubbed
excellence, or with butter, salty. Sweet

potatoes! Dear new knobbly ones, beside the oiled sides
of meaty carrots. Yes, carrots. Even you, dumplings,

with indigestible honey, treacle-streaky things. You
tongue-burners. You stodgy darlings. Tumbled out of the Marks
and Spencers tin or Mr. Kipling silver paper wrapper, warm and
ready except in summer. Cold strawberry sauce, cream and
raspberries. O sour gooseberry pie, dissemble nothing, squeezed
essence

of good juice. Joy in lieu of jelly at children's
parties, cow-heel that gives the horn a man seeing my
twelve-year-old buttocks oiled in hospital by a nurse assured me,
dirty

old bugger. I eat my six chosen slices of bread,
well-buttered, remembering you and your successor the tramp who
stole a book for me. Cracked

coffee cup of the lucky day, betokening mother-love,
nostalgic. Fill with Nescafé and milk for me. It is all great,
sick-making allure of old food, sentiment of the belly. I fill
with aniseed's

parboiled scagliola, porphyry of the balls. With, O
with, licorice, thin straws of it in sherbert, sucked up,
nose-bursting explosives of white powders! Yes,

montage of pre-European Turkish delights obtained under
the counter in wartime, or during periods of crisis, and

O the English sickness of it. Food, I adore you.
Pink-faced and randy! Come to me, mutton chops. Whiskers of
raw chicken-bones, wishes

and plastic cups. Unpourable Tizer. Take me before I
salivate. I require your exotic fineness, taste

of the English people, sweep me off my feet into
whiteness, a new experience. With beer. And with blue twists of
salt in the chip packets. Grease of newspaper. Vinegar of the
winter nights holding hands in lanes after *The Way To The Stars.*
It

is all there. Such past and reticence! O such
untranslatable grief and growing pains of the
delicate halibut. The heavy cod, solid as gumboots. And the
wet haddock, North Sea lumber of a long Tuesday's lunch. Fish
and

sauce. Nibbles and nutshells. Gulps of draught ale,
Guinness or cider made with steaks. English food, you are all
we have. Long may you reign!

AMELIA'S WILL

Where was Amelia's Will, and what was in it?
After the funeral, but not long after,
These were the questions her four sisters pondered
And three came to Amelia's cottage demanding
Answers to. Anne came with her sharp wit,
Alice with a hammer, Agnes with paper. Gwen,
Gwen thought there *was* no Will, and what was in it,
If there had been one, would have shocked them sadly,
So Gwen just came to watch.

                    Well, now, the search for it
Started quite well. First they evacuated
A ton of anthracite from the cellar, some pounds
Of coffee, flour, snuff, sugar and other powders
(Into which paper might have been ground) from the larder
And a quantity of ash from the kitchen grate.
That layer of dust along the banister
Gwen pointed out, none thought seemed thick enough,
So it was left. All yielded no results,
Though examined with great care through powerful lenses
For the imprint of invisible ink or fingers.

Where could the Will be? They grew violent.
Alice knocked bricks out from the front porch. Anne
Pulled at hall plaster with implacable anger.
And Agnes snapped four planks in the kitchen floor.
But no Will could be found, nor one deduced
From these concrete particulars, or others
Produced by such firm violence of three sisters.

Gwen kept her counsel. In the rocking-chair
Amelia loved to rock in by her window
That overlooked the lake, Gwen knitted socks
With pins she'd brought to soothe her flurried nerves.
They were soon needed. Anne lit a fire in
The dining-room and burned Amelia's nightie.
Alice shook all her books out and poured water

Over what Gwen thought was a fine collection
Of works on cookery. And Agnes screamed
Improper words no decent girl would whisper
In Gwen's opinion.

But things went too far
When cowed Saltpetre had to spring for life
To the linen cupboard to escape Anne's murderous
Jab with a carver. "How could *he* have swallowed
Amelia's Will?" Gwen cried. "Be reasonable.
Why must you all behave like mad beasts? Really."

But her three sisters in frustrated rage
No longer sought Amelia's Will. Gwen's blood,
Sweet blood of reason, pleased their palates more
Than absent paper bound in scarlet ribbon.
So Anne tipped back Gwen's graceful rocking-chair
And broke her spine. And Alice cut her up.
And Agnes found, set slantwise in her spleen,
A dart of paper, their Amelia's Will,
Which said: "I leave my sisters all I have,
Anne shall have Gwen, and Alice Anne..."
But here,
Concluding what would happen just in time
To greet Anne's body with a grim composure,
Agnes broke off, and snipped the Will in two.

So two old ladies with a cowed red cat
Spend nights in Devon with their bedroom lights on
Glaring like polished silver at each other.

A ROMAN DEATH

Folded alive in my slate sarcophagus
Bare as a grilled sole, watching the red spray
    Drenching the fine crow's-feet in my groin, I
    Feel a slow, sensuous pleasure. I think how

Tender and salt in the furred scum my bleached skin
Looks. Where the blood runs curdling the spilled oil, I
    Seem to see creambursts forced up through chilled wine to
    Crown my life's long feast. Fatigued by the steam, sweat

Spheres on my grooved brow. The knit scar's flash glares
Mauve in the brass where that crossed whore's flinstone
    Dented my oiled hair. She hated my nerve. When I
    Reeled in the park's dim fish-pond, my sunk limbs

Bunched like a peach-stone in wine. I was fished out,
Fated to die in my bath stretched flat, though. I
    Think of that young Jew. Confused by the plaice-white
    Blur of my limp creased flesh in the torch-flare,

How could "His" quaint views cure me? I once caught a
Black widow crawling on this drained floor. When I
    Rapped the rough walls with my jet ring, she ran straight
    Down to the wound of the waist-hole. I wonder

Whether she knew she was done for? The death-wish
Thins my desire in this flesh-fumed vault to a
    Shiver in air. I have shrunk like a cut flower and
    Wither in water. Am I, then, the first man

Scooped from the pit of his senses to die on a
Night of arranged swords? I spit on your furled, stiff
    Standards: my splashed walls are all I bequeath Rome. I
    Write: that about the sixth hour, in a wierd heat,

Drawn by the small room's brilliance, a caught bat
Flopped through the brass grille and smacked on the grey scum

Face up, whose cracked furred wings threshed blood all
Over the grey flagged walls and the beaked roof

Carved with its black hawks. The fire in my will spreads,
Fanned by the draught to a fierce flame. I wrench back,
Scratching my last grave, wavering verse, to
Shatter the bat's thin skull with my strigil.

MISSILE COMMANDER

I guess to be spending one's time
splitting cherry-stones into iced
water (counting how many float
and how many sink) might not seem

a task of much high reward for
an ex-Colonel of Infantry
on a missile site. No, sir. But
do you know what better way there

is of keeping a sound fit mind
in a guaranteed, processed-steel,
crap-proof bunker protected from
any shit but a direct hit

on Texas? I can tell you there's
a clear blue eye and a fine stiff
upper lip needed for spitting
cherry-stones. Yes, sir. Do you know

that in twelve days, allowing one
spit at dinner one spit at lunch
per day, the current score (just for
the record) is *nearly seven*

*hundred and thirty three up for one
hundred and eighty two down?* I
guess in Georgia those red bastards
are pushing around one sixty

five now. According to our checked
latest reports they sure are hard
on our heels. So if you'll excuse
my rudeness I'll just stick with my

conviction we can keep our nose
ahead of those Russkies only

through constant vigilance by our
little bowl of white cherry-stones.

DUST MAN

Over London fly
The super-flies.
If you get stung by one
Your memory dies.

> *I don't remember*
> *The days before the flies.*
> *I can't see for*
> *The motes in my eyes.*
> *But I ain't goin'*
> *Where the rubbish lies.*

I got one
With a pesticide
But it blew my mind
Before it died.

> *I don't remember*
> *The days before the flies.*
> *I can't see for*
> *The motes in my eyes.*
> *But I ain't goin'*
> *Where the rubbish lies.*

I clear the bins
With a sense of dread,
If one sees you,
You end up dead.

> *I don't remember*
> *The days before the flies.*
> *I can't see for*
> *The motes in my eyes.*
> *But I ain't goin'*
> *Where the rubbish lies.*

CRAZY JANE'S A.B.C.

Illustrations by Robin Lawrie

A

A was an Asiatic attic
with an angular space
    in which a draught sat:

while little a
was a plume waving
    above an Alaskan hat.

ancient arable A
in agony ailed away

B

B had a brace of storeys
and a bay window
    in each one:

while little b
began a battle in Albania
    by obtaining a gun.

beautiful Burmese B
broke a brick in the sea

C

C was a Capital fellow,
crooked as a compass
    with Costa Rican lips:

while little c
was a chill crisp of a moon
    in Ecuador, in eclipse.

curious choleric C
caught a crab in his tea

D

D was a dirt-track rider
who drove upside down
    around a dome:

while little d
was the double of little b
    and drummed at the Hippodrome.

dramatic industrious D
did a dog to death in the Dee

E

E had the uneasy air
of being a trident
    Neptune had let slide:

while little e
eloped with an English eel
    on the ebb-tide.

eccentric and egg-headed E
emended each sentence with glee

F

F was a Douglas fir
with formidable branches
    at the front of his head:

while little f
drooped like a French willow
    and flounced in a lettuce-bed.

foliate friable F
favoured a few of the deaf

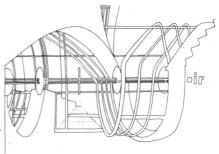

G

G was an egregious waiter
balancing a tray
    on his Greek hand:

while little g
groped in the gravy
    and thought life was Grand.

grave and ungodly was G
who grew a great weed on a flea

H

H was one of a pair
of horribly heavy
    TV aerial goals:

while little h
who played golf in Rugby
    hit them full of holes.

hardly a hot-head was H
who hoarded a ham in a hutch

I

I was inclined to be
irately ironic
    about the Isle of Wight:

while little i
spat a pip in the sky
    and ate Turkish delight.

indifferent Icarus I
had an icy but imbecile eye

J

J was a Mexican bird
with a blue crest
    and a jet foot:

while little j
was born in Djakarta
    and lived on jute.

jumping Jack J
ate juice and jam all day

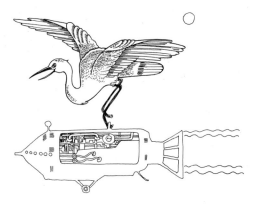

K

K was rather acute:
though he didn't look it,
    he was crowned like a king:

while little k,
his Viennese daughter,
    kissed him in The Ring.

cultural Kafkaesque K
kept cognac on a tray

L

L was a Saxon angle
reliably flat
    at one end:

while little l
lisped like a lounge lizard
    and lolled on lease-lend.

lissom elusive L
laid a loon's egg in a bell

M

M was an amnesty
which somebody granted
    under Malvern gables:

while little m
was kept muzzled
    in the livery stables.

magnificent Manchester M
managed to be one of them

N

N was a rather noble
little nothing
    I knew at Stonehenge:

while little n
ended up
    in a nunnery at Penge.

nasty and noxious N
was a nuisance to women and men

O

O was an oval pond
with an Oxford and Cambridge space
    for an ochre sun:

while little o
opened his mouth and froze
    at zero minus one.

Trucial Oman o
opted for all she could owe

P

P was a popinjay
from Polynesia
    in a plural pot:

while little p,
obsequiously Portuguese,
    lay below the line a lot.

proper and provident P
picked his nose with a pea

Q

Q was a queer sort of bird
from Queensland, Ontario,
   who queued for jail:

while little q
dipped his quill in Quince-juice
   and changed quetzal to quail.

iniquitous quarrelsome Q
dipped her Mary Quant toque in the stew

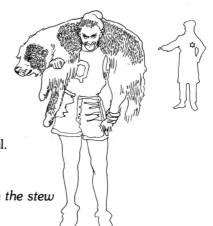

R

R was a Rhode Island ruffian
who always rode
   by the ridge of the rules:

while little r
who slurred his speech
   roughly suffered fools.

rollicking White Russian R
rumpled his ruff by the fire

S

S was a salamander
who singed the grass
    and hissed like a whip:

while little s
shimmied her way to Los Angeles
    in a comic strip

sibilant sinister S
Was assaulted by eels in Loch Ness

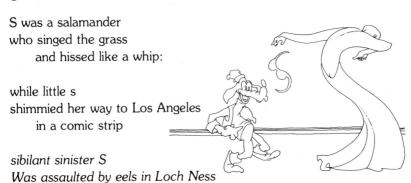

T

T was for trouble
always taking chances
    or up the Thames on a trip:

while little t
slipped in and out of the Trossachs
    with a few ties in a grip.

tremendously Topical T
toyed with a trifle of brie

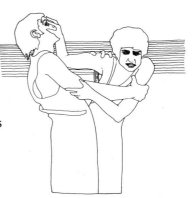

U

U was in Uruguay
much of the time,
    uxorious as an ox:

while little u
used to upbraid him in Urdu
    down by Chelsea Docks.

undulant uncle U
punched a trunk black and blue

V

V was a Vice-President,
invariable as St. Vincent
    and loveable as a vole:

while little v
was very vile
    and lived in a hole.

vicious invidious V
volubly veered through Tralee

W

W was a worn groove
in a Beatles record
    where the wind wormed with a will:

while little w
swigged away
    with a wicked snout at the swill.

Be-whiskered and weak W
washed at West Wycombe in glue

X

X was on Treasure Island
where they excavated the gold
    and x-rayed the enclosure:

while little x
was axed from Bootle's
    for an excruciating disclosure.

extravagant excellent X
exuded an odour of Trex

Y

Y was a Yale catapult
made of yucca wood
    who wouldn't hurt a fly:

while little y
yawned like a Yoruba
    when he was asked why.

*yodelling yoke-fellow Y
was used by a yak for a stye*

Z

Z was puzzled in Zanzibar
by the craze for zulus
    and was lazy enough to snore:

while little z
ran away with a zebra
    and grazed in a drug-store.

*zo-ological Zen-Buddhist Z
was led by a zombie to bed*

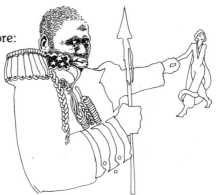

THE SILVER NEEDLE

a strip cartoon, for Sir Edward Coley
Burne-Jones (1833-1898)

(The story: *Attila, robot-knight of the Psychiatric Society, is again
invited to unravel a knot in the star-system of inner space. This time
it is the imperialism of a drug-ring, Hallucinogenics Unlimited, he is
briefed to combat. Their cult of primitivism and ritual pity, inspired
by the virgin queen, Medulla, is out of line with the normal sex-worship
orientation of the Planet 4 group and its ruling clique, the Table-men.
Attila is called by them, and flies to work, Now read on.)*

1   The Call of Attila.

From weeks of in-trays
he seethed to the lift. So
rose

through four orgasms
in the new Janssen feelie, flicked

the in-switch for a re-fill, swallowed
his testerosones and was out,

a fine blaze of Nuremberg
in his gas-suit, at ease

before the Table-men. A million eggs
on a flat glass disc
reflecting
eyed him. *You are called, Attila,*

the scent whispered, undulant
from the green orifice
below the glitter. Tickled,

scintillant, in a whirl
of Semen Number 5 (those

46

thigh-borne odours!)

his nerves grovelled
for the job. *Lord, I am thine:*
O.K., boss: Mein Fuehrer

brimmed through his lips
until the voice-pointer
answered the gyroscope

and he was back in the televator
conditioned, ready
for a new grail

to be wrenched
out of the misery of the pitied.

2   *Attila And The Grey Sisters.*

Years later, in the burned egg, the
man-womb of elaborate alloys
Planet 4 had long since riveted
to his watch-bone

and made contractible for a
vitamin pill (b c g and z)

or expandable to a space-ship
with a range of nine star-systems,

Attila took stock. Happy
to be again on a voyage, playing

time-charades, eating
engine-oil and imagining
flexible metal Brunnhildas,

there was lots to do. And apt,
four-fifths sexual fantasy as it was,
to the job in hand. So flowed

the long days, clouds arcing
past the glass on the phone-screen, a
sense of sea, clouds, islands
infusing all that was. It was good

to be a robot, alone,
and like a man again. Except that outside

(and Attila knew it)
the piercing rays of the Table-men,

assuming form, like the grey sisters,
ever circled,

swooping and following,

waiting for the mission to be accomplished
or the next hero to be substituted

that the great work not falter
but go on.

3   *The Finding of Medulla.*

The whole
strangled beach was alive
with subjected catatonics

when Attila tuned in. They
were celebrating

something he'd heard of — Christomide —
a white child without arms

lifted out of the mud

to a blazing Orion 3. It was holding
a sugar-cube in its teeth and

bit hard when the hero
immolated it
with his anode-gun. So much

for the gospel of love, he thought, but
heresy
has got to be hurt. So Attila

ever-leaping her prone vassals,
approached Medulla, our Lady
of LSD,

locked on her oil throne
in acid light, unutterable green

beyond the hand of man. And on her skin,
against her right side, the
silver needle shone.

4   The Rock of Doom

To receive, point-blank
from nothing, urges of intuition

along the space-orb, with a rare chance
of the big O
approaching, is a fierce irritant

to the sloth's testicles, magnetic mines,
of a space-man. So Attila,

between the legs of Destiny, the goddess
Medulla,
fussed by the onset of rigor sexualis mortis,

destroyed precious machinery
(P ration, box three)
for seven aeons

before he could trust his hands
to clap on the nose-phones
and inhale the message.

Androyeda needs you, the
scent breathed. *She is chained
to a rock.*

Waves lap, the granite
penis rears: the bared girl
                              .

rattles her chains below the varnish and,

slipping off his helmet, the
hero is down with a clank

of reassuring metal. *Hold tight, sister,*
he snaps and is up

and chopping her off before
the small town in the background
wakes up. Reeling

it back in the 4D
screen in his head
Attila wonders

just what he's missing. He flicks
his switches: yes,
the monster.

5   *The Doom Fulfilled.*

The monster. Pervasive
as an echo, stronger

50

than kettledrums, magnetic

to the nerve-ends of heroic metal, it
coils, spitting

a strange gas in his eyes. Attila
feels its thongs in his groin as
he hacks, helmeted,

breast-plated. Behind him
the greedy buttocks

of Androyeda turn
towards the cameras. She is open

to man or beast. Despite the
circling Furies, the

whole bleak glass
in the Planetarium of nothingness,

Attila has finished. The
thing is dead. Filing its
biological structure

in the back pocket of his
archive-wallet, he

lapses, under the eager toes

of the nymphomaniac Androyeda,
into a dream.

Attila dreams.

6   *The Baleful Head.*

And in his dream Attila
flew back
to complete his earlier mission. The

dark head was there on the beach
where the screwed bones waited, the
bowed blind heads of the watchers
and the thing all needed

though none had the wit
to lift it clear.

Attila was walking
over the pebbles, hearing
the space-mind
(or was it the wind?) keening.

Attila was lifting
(drawing back the snake-hair)
the silver needle,

that pure beam of endless light.

Raising the totem
towards the star
Attila knew what the catatonics meant
by reviving Christomide.

The wind shrilled
with the cries of a million
dissolved in history.

And Attila bent
to replace it
for a single split-second

before the grey sisters
dived

and the silver needle blazed again
into the desperate circle of the damned

always in power

IV

THE GREEDY BOOK

I

The book ate up the whole of the Director General's
    green tea.
It ate up the borzois.
It ate up a wombat and a telephone directory.

There were no new numbers.

It ate up the world of Enid Blyton, and the era
    of Isaac Newton, in monochrome.
It ate nutshells and sherbet.
It ate the island of Dogs and the core of a
    grapefruit and the style of Thomas Merton.

There was no stopping it.

It belched, and there were free-ways.
It farted, and the juice of Monday stewed in a
    fine mess of *Borodent*.

II

So far, so bad.
The book was angry.
It ate the grubby endpapers of Newcastle, the
    dry docks and the dog-eared stowaways from Peru.

It knew.
They were after it.

The book ate up the police and the crow's nest.
It ate the iron in the soul.
It ate Tuesday.

Who was to blame?
Were you?

The book went to the lavatory four times before
    matins.
It peeed on the tiled floor of Sir Edward Kennedy, Bart.,
    at Tewkesbury.
It was very bad.

III

The book paused.
It was still hungry

It dug its teeth in the soft flesh of a
    bunch of news-boys.
It ground them to pulp.

It spewed grey matter on the hoardings of
    Flanders and South Vietnam.
It egged itself on.

The book took a run at a high rise of ice cream
    Sundays and gulped down their format.
It gulped down their hindmat, too, and the North
    side of the tenements in St Albans.

It guzzled ice-floes and flotillas.
It gave them a hard time.

IV

The book was greedy.
It needed food.

Nutrition! Nutrition! it shouted, as it
    waved its arms for a waiter.
It ate volubly.
It ate water.

The book grew hot with its own energy as it
    swallowed.
It masticated.
It threw chicken bones at the Great Wall
    of China.

It ground down the Houses of Parliament to a
    fine powder.
Politicians ran in and out of its ears like
    peppermints.

It blinked, and its eyes grew even bigger than
    its stomach.
It took in krill, and it had a whale of
    a time.

V

The book became full.
Its mouth moved more slowly.

It ate only the topsides of little nougats
    and grilled sundries.
It ground towards a halt.

Was it nauseated?
The book was a force of Nature, it needed
    more.

It began to evacuate.
It sat on its piece of porcelain with a bride
    and a sandwich,
It itched its parts.

When the book was finished, it buckled its belt
    with a flourish.
It rose to its full stature and called
    for a soup.

The book was greedy.

It started again, its messy hands dug in the world
    for more meat.
It began to eat.
It was never satisfied.

BADGER'S POEM

The badger ran rapidly down the
    thick walk, snuffling.
Eee, eee, eee, he cried, when he stopped.

He was a good badger.

Very sleek were his incurved paws, and his
    lean snout.
His belly, very commodious.

He was a good eater, was this badger.
Worms, worms, and more worms.

His stomach was a veritable cauldron of worms.

Anyway, apart from that.

Why are you writing a poem about this little
    furry obnoxious badger?

He isn't obnoxious.

O? Well, they say he is.
Out West, they're killing him in hundreds.

With guns. With poison gas. With vicious dogs.
And (for all I know) with trained weasels.

Poor badger.
I wouldn't like to be him.

Even if I was as bad as they say he is.

I should expect a better deal.

So I'm putting this particular badger in a poem.
To commemorate his glossy appearance, and his

neat nocturnal habits.

Very like in fact those of an English gentleman
    on his way to a dinner party.
The sort of English gentleman who is presently
    massacring his kind with dogs etc.

Eee, eee, eee, he cried, when he stopped.
And I'll bet you would, too.

ELEPHANTS NEVER FORGET, AND MICE DON'T EITHER

Stratford came from Stratford.
Yesterday.
Well, almost.

Hamley is older.
Hamley is really about the oldest new thing you
  could imagine.

They both live in the usual nutshell.
Up at five, do the chores and back to bed for a
  nice snooze before breakfast.

Hamley is bigger. Well, really he's smaller.
Also, Hamley is she.

Not like Chi-Chi.
She.

Hamley is very fastidious about her little
  white apron.
Every day she washes it in rat's milk.

Stratford is hard and pink.
A lot of the time he gallops about with his nose
  in the air reviewing invisible troops.

Stratford would like to be the General.
Not just a General, the General.

Anyway, they both get on very well together.
So far.

I don't promise what will happen when the
  sun comes out.
Stratford has that faraway look in his eyes already.

Hamley is gnashing her stew-bones.

Watch out, Stratford.
You're in for breakfast.

I BOUGHT

I bought an egg.
I bought a mink and a substitute.
I bought a mild-mannered starling.
I bought.

I bought a wig with blue buckles and a dromedary
    crying mercy.
I bought an alarm-clock.
I bought the nose of a pig with a green armature
    in it.
I bought a white fowl.

I bought a sacristy in Afghanistan.
I bought a mole.
I bought the ecstatic mother of a monk selling
    strawberries in a rabbit's nest.

I bought the ear of Medusa.
I bought you.
I bought you a trio of sandscrapers.
I bought you a night.
I bought you the world squatting under the
    eye of a toadstool.
I bought you mice.

Here are the mice I bought.
Here are the new snowshoes and the paper
    owl.
Here is the eye.

Here is the broken arrow in love with the sexual
    possibilities of the whitebait.
Here is the world.

Use it.

Here is the nut cracker.
Here is the poem.
Here is the crimson account-book of the man who
    bought the Philosophy Museum.

He bought a wink and a dog with no hair.
He bought a seed.
He bought a violent whistle and the nuisance value
    of toothache.
He bought a bear.

He put them in a sacred earwig dripping with
    gnat's honey and vaseline.
He put them for you.

Take them.

Sell them for what will buy a Canadian stove and
    a money jug.
Sell them for broken china and Mu tea.
Sell them for me.

Buy me with elephants and a brick igloo.
Buy me with pink shoes.
Buy me with a rattle and a hamster.
Buy me with all the gold in the nest of the
    last winter seal.

Buy me with you.

THE JOURNEY TO THE ISLAND

I

Where shall we go?

Shall we go to the Hopalong Cassidy Festival in Bangkok?
Shall we go to the mundane side of the High Sierra?

No, let's go to the island.

Shall we go to the Bumper Island?
Shall we go to the island of mugs?

Let's go to the island surrounded by musing water
    on the crucible of Venus.
Let's go to the Slice Island.
Let's go to the braking island where all the cars
    grow plasticine.

All right.

Shall we go to the island by complicated machinery?
Shall we go on clouds, or by ankle?
Shall we go with a wire devil and a pint of Ribena?

Let's go by Tuesday.

We'll go by Crewe.
We'll go with a plaque of oars and a knot of
    rumbustious toe-nails.
We'll go with a flu epidemic and Genghis Khan.

Let's not.
Let's go with a Greyhound bus and a Maserati
    superior.

The monks will like that.

They will.

II

We packed.

In the boot of the car we packed a magpie and a strainer.
We packed wheels and knee-caps.
We packed a mole's ear in the spare tyre and a
    duodenum of mercury in the radiator.

We packed sounds of fishing.
We packed snores for a spare owl and a mood
    of compassion.

We packed a litter-box and a meal of Candy.
Under the back-axle we packed a glittering new
    spine-chiller distracted by orange sauce
    on the Freeway.

We packed.

And, after we finished packing, we unjointed the
    carburettor and went to sleep.

P.S.

We hid the key to the Orangery in the sump.
It was fun.

III

On the road we encountered muslin.
It lay in the ditch and sweated profusely.

After the second turning, we drove through a village
    strident with grass-hoppers in labour.
The mules reeked of offal.
Broken sawdust rose up from the gutters and doffed
    its fourteen gallons of hats.

We held our noses.

We held our arm-bands and the belts of our
    flushed satchels.

Durable amnesties were available.
We caught them.

Later, the Motorway filled up with determined parasols
    and the otters were more careful.

We reached Falmouth.

IV

On the sea, the boat rocked like a whistle.
Little waves crept into the fresh majorities
    of the timbers.

We smelled ozone.
We smelled fire in the wind and the clay of
    obtuse skuas in the cliffs.

We moved fast.

The island loomed in the breeze and we breakfasted
    on sundae.

It was cheap.

V

The monks were in signatures of vellum.
They ate mincemeat.
On the backs of their hands they took scrolls
    of satin underwear and wrote an admission ticket.

We went in.

We saw the barrels of bubble-gum.
We saw the witch of Cirencester.
We took the cure in a bottle.

The monks wangled and made sherbet.

They threw a party into the brass oven.
They iced nutshells.

They took the moon from the corner of a manuscript
and the stars from a sundial.

It was good news.

VI

On the way back, we saw white snails in the
hedge-rows.
It was Pisces weather.

We saw the sky milked for Armagnac.
We saw the glue in the crow.
We saw Nefertiti handled by snowmen.

It was awful.

Sleep came later, bowling along the raw butter
of Dartmoor.

At Flaw Edge, it was cold.
At Arundale, it was only nineteen minutes to
Christmas.

We came home.

VII

Dream of it, then, later, whatever it was.

Dream of the roebuck and the vigilant ant.
Remember the larder of torture and the
dungeon of honey.

Dream of the whales.
Dream of the big hound with his ear-rings.
Dream of the stone that when you licked it made
the sun blink in motes of garnet.

Row into sleep.
Dream there of the octopus.
He will come and hold the world in his
    glossy claws.

Lay the egg on his brow.
Stroke him with grace, and with power.

It is an exercise.

Be perfect in it.
Be all that you want to be.

Sleep well now, and dream.

It is Easter.

V

THE CARNATION-MAN
a fragment, after Ponge

I

And was it easy
to be so balanced?
To be always an

exfoliation
of exact petals
above the same cane —

peaceable amidst
so many sabres —
and with such clear thorns

upsetting oneself
into bloom, as it
were, a pure model

of tense poise! Beyond

II

the shocked summerhouse
where the bloated lips

of poison trumpets
swallowing their own
and other people's

tails, reminded one
of his attachment
to rage, I watched him

dissolving into
emanations of
cool mint.

III

As the cane

tapped a green knee-cap
and buttons below
the uncut stubble

cleft into acres
of matching suds one
sensed the violence.

IV

To be split into
seven letters, an
alphabet of

atrocious thatch!
And all those clacking
tongues in the sunk

conservatory!
Such wet satin! So
many pink faces!

One's carnation-man
was never of much
account if two white

fingers could hold him.

THE AIRSHIP POEM

After the other words
had lined up and gone into
their complicated arks
and envelopes
I was left with the baggy
silk of the airship
poem, that spent elephant,
still wheezing
in the breeze.

I let it ride
for too long on its
title. It never floated
easily above images
that bogged it down. It was
always a slow
starter.
The airship poem
never got off the ground.

So I formally decide
tonight to abandon
the airship poem
and let it down
with a sense of guilt
mixed with relief.
Dreaming, though,
that it might rise
and soar still

grey-lavender
above Richmond Park
and fly with 26
or perhaps 30
stanzas,
all rhyming
on awkward words,

and in a rare metre,
inflating indolence.

EVENING PRIMROSES

In the sun, all day,
They pose, furled as in
Rust sheaths, fighting heat's
Abrasive brilliance,
Restrained exemplars.

Later, each opens
Pale into darkness,
Cool twilight, semen-
Scented, shallow fires,
Mute incandescence.

Already, in tight
Whirled cases, red-streaked,
Others beside them
Are assembling in
Volted secure time

It seems. But they burn
Once only, exposed
Scooped hollows, veined
As with age, breaking
Towards the moon. See,

Heroes of subdued
Light, how far, advanced
On green, one rises
Hour after black hour
Out of ground, in air!

All night, laid open
As in bed, virgin
To the white pour of
Moth-light, they flame in
Obscure, wounded pride.

Afterwards, at dawn,

Each turns, sensing there
Is no time, to furl
As a flag, indrawn,
Doused in the raw glare.

Failing, each falls, curled
As by heat, stained
With a cold radiance,
Darkened yellows, dipped
In a stiff manure.

And still, far back, sap
As a driven wind
Under their stigma,
Nosed essence, others
Grope, torn, into being.

BUYING A HEART

I consider: that, if she were to
take it out of the deep-freeze less than
bone-hard, frozen muscle, it would prick

my conscience, bleed through newsprint, and be
a burden; but that, as things are, though
it ran the blood of an ox for two

years, and weighs nearly half of what will
eat it, now that it is no longer
a pump, and chills my fist, I have to

accept the disquieting thought of
inevitable change, whether I
like it or not; and that, even if

my own slow heart, which is a pretty
doubtful affair, were to beat faster
in frightened sympathy, there is just

nothing this one could do about it
at all, since it is now entirely
dead. It has a new destiny, which

is to grow wet in the sun, stay cold
in another refrigerator
and satisfy one cat for one week.

MAXIMS OF BLUEBEARD

I

Cleaning an electric razor
Feels like oiling a tractor
After centuries of mucking out.

II

Not feeling musical
I hanged her with piano-wire
From a button-hook.

III

Once round or twice I thought
Depending on which you want to put out:
The fire or an eye.

IV

Neither of us was raining
When I put my umbrella
Down her throat.

V

Somebody tell me:
Why does the water clot
When I take its temperature?

VI

Imagine a wasp
You could roll back
And extract the sting from!

VII

I only pulled
My nails off
To make room for these blades.

THIS IS THE DAY

I
This is the day
when the traffic stops,
all its golden horns
blazing in the circuses
    to please your name

This is the day

II
This is the day
when the little flowers
walk to the gates
of the parks, singing
    all their perfumes
    to your neck and bones

This is the day

III
This is the day
when the white polar bears
wash their paws
quietly
    in the zoo
    while you lie sleeping

This is the day

IV
This is the day
when the marmoset,
the creature of evil,
closes his book of blame
    and lets you through

for all time

This is the day

V
This is the day
when the moon
rises
over the cliff-tops of London
    sweet as a white owl
    to breathe in peace for you

This is the day

VI
This is the day
when the stars
have a rival,
all those jewelled names
    racing in air
    to meet your needs

This is the day

VII
This is the day
when the years open
their boxes,
doves fluttering gently
    over the many facets
    of your future

This is the day

VIII
This is the day
when all your friends
chiming like clocks
speak the same hour,
    one for you

to live and blossom in

This is the day

IX

This is the day
when the post-cards
drop into the letter-boxes
very softly
in case you wake
too soon

This is the day

X

This is the day
when all is well,
exquisite weather
sounding
through all the funnels
of the steamers in the Thames

This is the day

XI

This is the day
when nothing needs to be done
except to say
this is the day
this is the day

This is the day